1 MONTH OF
FREE
READING

at
www.ForgottenBooks.com

By purchasing this book you are eligible for one month membership to ForgottenBooks.com, giving you unlimited access to our entire collection of over 1,000,000 titles via our web site and mobile apps.

To claim your free month visit:
www.forgottenbooks.com/free955019

ISBN 978-0-260-54108-6
PIBN 10955019

This book is a reproduction of an important historical work. Forgotten Books uses
state-of-the-art technology to digitally reconstruct the work, preserving the original format
whilst repairing imperfections present in the aged copy. In rare cases, an imperfection in
the original, such as a blemish or missing page, may be replicated in our edition. We do,
however, repair the vast majority of imperfections successfully; any imperfections that
remain are intentionally left to preserve the state of such historical works.

FINANCIAL STATEMENT

OF THE

1885

ON. A. M. ROSS.

TORONTO:

PRINTED BY "GRIP" PRINTING AND PUBLISHING COMPANY.
1885.

FINANCIAL STATEMENT

OF THE

HON. A. M. ROSS.

TORONTO:

PRINTED BY "GRIP" PRINTING AND PUBLISHING COMPANY.

1885.

FINANCIAL STATEMENT.

OF THE

HON. A. M. ROSS.

LEGISLATIVE ASSEMBLY,
TORONTO, Friday, 13th Feb., 1885.

MR. SPEAKER,—Before making the motion with which I shall conclude, it is my duty on the present occasion to lay before the House the financial position of the Province for the past year, and to state what have been our receipts and expenditures, what are our requirements for the coming year (for the present year, rather), and also to make such references to any financial transactions of the Province as may appear necessary to give the House a full understanding as to how the Province stands financially. First I will lay before the House our receipts for the past year, 1884, which have been as follows :—

RECEIPTS FOR 1884.

Dominion of Canada :—

Subsidy	$1,116,872 80	
Specific Grant	80,000 00	
		$1,196,872 80
Interest on Capital held, and debts due by the Dominion to Ontario	$207,903 86	
Interest on investments	57,521 79	
		265,425 65
Crown Lands Department		570,305 41
Algoma Taxes		2,215 85
Education Department	$37,069 35	
do School of Practical Science	900 00	
		37,969 35
Law Stamps		66,599 98
Licenses		211,353 71
Drainage Works Assessments		23,618 37

Public Institutions :—

Toronto Lunatic Asylum.	$29,990 33	
London do do	10,335 18	
Hamilton do do	4,024 98	
Kingston do do	3,319 38	
Orillia do do	1,916 10	
Reformatory for Females	3,808 37	
do do Boys...................	618 39	
Central Prison	53,615 57	
Deaf and Dumb Institute................	583 38	
		$108,211 68

Casual Revenue :—

Fines, etc......................	$4,776 29	
Surrogate Court Fees...................	616 00	
Division do do	4,449 68	
County do do	964 10	
Insurance Co's. Fees......	450 00	
Official Gazette.......................	9,792 06	
Ontario Statutes.......................	524 54	
Private Bills	3,800 00	
Provincial Secretary's Department........	7,389 80	
Incidentals.....	663 98	
		33,426 45
Municipal Loan Fund		4,476 20
Kingston L. A. Cap. Acct.................................		753 36
Lock-up, Rat Portage, do		20 00
Mimico Farm do		625 60
Agricultural and Arts Association, *re* alterations Agricultural		
Hall		2,000 00
		$2,523,874 41
Drainage Debentures........................		46,037 37

Annuities :—

Proceeds of Sale of $13,400 of 40-year		
annuities	$248,191 71	
5 per cent. interest on $119,058 84, de-		
posited to meet December certificates...	2,451 96	
		250,643 67
Total		$2,820,555 45

Now, hon. gentlemen will notice that I have made the classification a little different in this statement of receipts from that
which appeared in former statements laid before the House ; thus,
instead of including the interest on the funds held by the Dominion as part of the subsidy, I have taken it into interest account,
to which it properly belongs, as interest on funds held to the
credit of the Province.

There are one or two matters in this statement to which I wish to draw the attention of the House. In the first place, it will be noticed by those hon. members who have the statement of last year in their possession as to what our anticipated receipts were, that we have received less by $81,038.78 than we anticipated. Last year I referred to the deficiency in our Crown Lands revenue of 1883, explaining that we were then deficient by the sum of $114,000 in what we had expected to receive from that source, and calling the attention of the House to the fact that it was owing to the depression in the lumber trade and the consequent reduction in the amount received from timber dues at that time. In making up our estimates for 1884, we hoped that we would see an improvement in the year's operations, and we therefore estimated that we would receive a larger sum than what we realized in the previous year. I am sorry to say, however, that that depression in the lumber interest has continued, in fact has become rather more intensified than it was at that time, and therefore there is a still further reduction in the revenues from that source.

We estimated that our receipts from the different sources of Crown Lands revenue would be $690,000, whilst they have only been $570,305, or a deficiency in our revenue from that Department of $119,695. Considering, Mr. Speaker, that during the past year we have been passing through a period of depression which I think is acknowledged upon all hands to have been more severe than we have experienced for many years; considering that that depression, that dulness in trade, has existed not only in our own Dominion but in England and the United States, with whom we have large trade relations, I think, Sir, that taking these circumstances into consideration, the amount that we have received from that source may be considered very fair, although much less than we had anticipated.

Mr. MEREDITH.—I would ask the hon. gentleman if the arrears due by the holders of timber limits are more than they have been previously?

Hon. Mr. Ross.—I made the same enquiry myself. I believe that they are, although I have not the figures to give the House. I believe it is the practice of the Crown Lands Department not to collect the dues, even although the timber is cut, until it is disposed of or shipped, and in consequence of the depression, and the lumbermen not being able to dispose of their lumber, the arrears are, I believe, larger than they would otherwise have been.

There are some lesser fluctuations in regard to the receipts to which it will not be necessary to call attention. However, I daresay the House would like to know how our anticipations have been realized in regard to revenues from licenses. We anticipated a revenue from licenses of $200,000. It will be seen that we have received no less than $211,353.71. From the statement that has been handed in to me by the officers of the License Department, it appears that our estimated revenue, which was based upon the amount we might receive from Ontario licenses alone, has been very nearly exactly what we anticipated. The amount derived from the issue of licenses issued by the Ontario Board was $200,-949.93, and we received in addition $10,403.90 from licenses issued by the Dominion Board, making the total of $211,353.71. The statement shows that the Dominion licenses were principally confined to ordinary hotel and shop licenses. There were issued under the Ontario Board 3,217 hotel licenses, and 182 by the Dominion Board. The number of shop licenses issued by the Ontario Board was 666, and by the Dominion Board 14.

It will also be noticed in the statement of receipts, that we have a new item which did not appear in our former statements of Provincial revenues, viz., the amount of $250,643.67 from the sale of annuities authorized under the statute of last session. This amount is the proceeds of the sale of forty years' annuities of the amount of $13,400 per annum, sold since that time, under that Act. Tenders were asked for the purchase of those annuities, and it was asked that the tenders should be for annuities payable either in Canada or England. The most favourable was one received where the amount was made payable in Canada, and it was accepted, the rate being at a small fraction below 4½ per cent., say 4½ per cent. (Hear, hear.) Last year when I introduced this matter, in making my financial statement, I stated that I anticipated that that would be about the rate at which we would be able to sell our annuities, and I will quote my language on that occasion :

"The Government believe they can issue new certificates upon a basis, at the very highest, of 4½ per cent. interest. From enquiries I have made I find those now in existence, which were based upon 6 per cent., are being sold and negotiated to give the purchaser a rate of only 4½ per cent. I therefore think we are safe in saying we will be able to issue new certificates on a basis of 4½ per cent."

That statement of what our expectations were was accepted by the House as satisfactory, at least, no exception was taken as to the price stated as likely to be realised. The price we have obtained has been a very fair one, but at the same time if we have to place future securities on the market, of the same character, I expect that we shall be able to do still better. It may be asked why we have adopted the annuity plan. Well, sir, one reason is, and we think it is a reason that actuates most municipal institutions, that it is better to have a portion of these securities falling due each year, and by that means avoid the trouble and expense of keeping account of and re-investing sinking funds. We conceive that the doing of this saves expense and cost connected with these sinking funds, which are items of considerable importance. It has been contended by some that it would have been better, and that we would have been able to realise a better price for the securities, had we issued them for an amount sufficient to take up the whole of the outstanding railway certificates, viz., something over $2,000,000. That, I say, has been contended, and that by doing so we should have been able to sell them in England for a better price than we obtained in this country. Now such a proposition, Mr. Speaker, would not, I think, commend itself either to the House or to the country. It was never intended, as I explained when I introduced the measure, that we should, every year, take up these railway certificates by the issue of fresh annuities. That was not necessarily to be the case. It was only, as I explained then, that from year to year as a deficiency in our revenue might exist, we might, if necessary, renew these certificates by the issue of new ones, but in any year in which the receipts might be sufficient to retire the old certificates, they might be taken up as heretofore and paid out of our Consolidated Revenue Fund. It would therefore have been very unwise to have issued new certificates for the whole of those falling due, some of them not for eighteen years to come, merely for the purpose of getting a large loan placed on the London market, and having the securities quoted upon the stock exchange there. Another objection to that course would be, that we know that the rate of interest is growing less year by year. We know that a few years ago the Dominion Government was obliged to pay 6 per cent. on loans made to them. We know that they are now getting their loans for 4 per cent.; nominally, the issue is at $3\frac{1}{2}$, but I believe the rate is really 4 per cent. The old certificates which were issued by authority of the House, and which we are now renewing, were based upon 6 per cent. upon the investment, while those we have been selling are at $4\frac{1}{2}$: It would be folly, therefore, to anticipate by a present issue the taking up of annuities not maturing for eighteen years to come, but it is only by doing so that we would have effected a loan of such magnitude as would enable us to place it upon the London stock exchange. I may mention also that we received tenders at the rate of $4\frac{3}{8}$ per cent. if the amounts had been payable in England, and it may be asked why we did not accept a higher tender payable in England instead of accepting a lower one payable in Canada. I think, sir, it will be obvious to everyone that it is much more advantageous, because we thereby escape many charges for commission, brokerage, etc., that we do not have to pay on those payable here. I say it is far better that we should have these certificates payable at the Treasurer's office here, and escape all those incidental charges which are connected with a loan payable out of this country. I may mention that at the present time the Dominion Government pay their financial agents a commission of one per cent. for the placing of all new loans. Besides that, they pay for brokerage, stamp duty, etc., one-half per cent. more; for all interest payable in England, one-half per cent.; on investments of sinking fund, three-fourths per cent.; and on redemption of loans, one per cent. In addition to that, they also pay any losses incurred in exchange, in remitting money either to or from England. Now all these commissions are saved to this Province by our having these securities payable here at the Treasurer's office, and all these things must be taken into account.

Mr. MEREDITH.—Does not the purchaser usually re-sell these securities on the English market?

Hon. Mr. ROSS.—I do not know whether they are re-sold or not, but that has no bearing on my argument. I am speaking of what charges would be entailed on the Province were we to make our loans payable there. If we did so, our interest would have to be remitted there, our debentures sold there, they would have to be redeemed there, and our sinking fund would have to be invested there.

Now, I may just as well say in regard to exchange, that I find that the Dominion Government remitted last year $5,116,790 to England, upon which they paid as exchange or discount $15,863, or three-tenths of one per cent. for the cost of transmitting the money there. Then a portion of their sales in England had to be brought to Canada to meet liabilities here. They drew on their agents in England to the extent of $3,815,100, and paid a discount of $28,499, or three-fourths per cent., for getting the money here. These are very serious and heavy charges, but the Dominion has to submit to them in consequence of making their loans payable in England. Besides that, I may mention that they maintain an officer there at a cost to the country last year of over $40,000, who, I believe, it was intended should relieve the Government from many of these charges, but he has not done so.

Now, Sir, as regards the price which we have obtained from the sale of these securities, I have looked at quotations of securities as published in the *Economist*, and I find that similar securities have been rated at about the same. I find, for instance, that Cape of Good Hope debentures bearing four and a half per cent. interest are sold on the English market at from 95 to 97 ; Mauritius bearing four and a half per cent. are sold at 102 ; I find that New Zealand debentures bearing four and a half per cent. are saleable at from 101 to 103 ; I find Quebec debentures bearing four and a half per cent. are saleable at from 101 to 103. These are all loans payable in England, and you will see that although there is a small premium to the extent of about one and two per cent., that would all be absorbed by the first cost of making the sale in England. So that I say, taking these as criterions, we have received as good a price as has been obtained even where they are payable in the old country.

There is one other item in the receipts to which I wish to draw the attention of the House. It is the item of interest derived from capital and debts held by the Dominion, $207,903.86. That amount hon. gentlemen will see is $71,207 more than we have received before. That was a half year's interest on funds placed to our credit by the Dominion and paid in July under the Act passed last year at Ottawa. It will be recollected that last year I drew the attention of the House, in referring to the accounts that had been submitted by the Dominion, to the fact that they had charged us interest on the excess of debt between 1867 and 1873, before that debt was assumed by the Dominion. It will be recollected that I contended that by the construction of the Act of 1873 we were entitled to be relieved from that interest as from the date of 1867. Hon. gentlemen will bear in mind that by the Confederation Act it was provided that the Dominion should become legally liable for the whole of the debts of the old Province of Canada, and that they should assume altogether and relieve the Province to the extent of $62,500,000. In 1873 it was found that the debt of the late Province of Canada amounted to $73,000,000, and upon application by some of the provinces an Act was passed relieving the provinces from that excess of debt, the Dominion assuming the whole. By the construction of that Act I claimed last year that the wording of it was really to relieve the provinces from the date of 1867 instead of from 1873, but in the accounts they have charged us with interest from 1867 to 1873, and I claimed that we ought to have credit to the extent of about $5,000,000, Ontario's share being over $2,500,000. Now that contention of mine was scouted at the time by hon. gentlemen opposite (hear, hear); they disputed the position I took. They stated "that it was a construction wholly unwarranted, and one not to be listened to for a moment." They said "that we had no possible right to the amount," and "that it would be a very gross breach of faith on the part of the Dominion if they were to grant it." Well, sir, I am glad to be able to inform the House that the interpretation which I placed upon that Act has been accepted by the Dominion Government (applause), and that the proportion of interest which had been charged against us in those accounts has been credited by the Dominion to Ontario in the sum of $2,882,289.

Mr. MEREDITH.—I suppose that is a case of Quebec domination?

Hon. Mr. FRASER.—No. It is Ontario justification.

Hon. Mr. ROSS.—Now, hon. gentlemen I suppose will contend that the interpretation which I put upon the Act was really not that accepted by the Dominion, but I think that if I read the Act passed in the Dominion House last session it will be clearly seen that it was so, in fact, the whole Act was based upon that contention. There would be no reason for it otherwise. It recites the Act of 1873, and is virtually an interpretation of that Act. The Act reads: "Whereas the subsidies payable under the British "North America Act, 1867, to the several provinces thereby united "into one Dominion respectively, were re-adjusted and increased "by the operation of the Act of the Parliament of Canada, 36 Vic.;

" chap. 30, but the said increase was allowed only on and from the
" first day of July, 1873, etc." Then it goes on to provide that
" in the accounts between the several provinces and the Dominion,
" the amounts by which the yearly subsidy to each was increased
" by the Act 36 Vic., chap. 30, shall be calculated and allowed to
" Ontario and Quebec (jointly, as having formed the late Province
" of Canada) as if the said Act had directed that such increase
" should be allowed from the day of the coming into force of ' The
" British North America Act, 1867.' " Now, that was my contention, that the Act itself stated that the amount named in the
British North America Act should be read as if the increased
amount was a part of the Act. It was upon that interpretation
and construction that we were to be relieved from that debt. I
say that the Dominion have accepted that interpretation. If this
was merely an act of grace, giving us an additional subsidy, there
would be no justification for giving it to Ontario and Quebec
jointly upon the basis of the division of debts as fixed by the
award, and not upon population. The equivalent that was given to
the three smaller provinces was given upon the basis of population. I say also there is no defence for the division that the Dominion Government has made between Ontario and Quebec except on
account of its being in connection with the debt due by the late
province, and because it was deemed to be a carrying out of the
intention of the Act of 1873.

Now, it was contended also by hon. gentlemen opposite that it
was not in the interests of the Province of Ontario to ask this,
because they contended that Ontario has to contribute from two-
thirds to three-fourths of the revenue of the Dominion, and therefore by making application for this increase, Ontario would be
contributing to the Dominion more, perhaps, than she would be
receiving if we only got our receipts in proportion to population.
That was the contention of hon. gentlemen opposite. But the
Dominion have imposed increased taxation within the last three
years, and have been able to claim that they have a surplus of receipts
of upwards of $17,000,000. The possession of that surplus revenue

has no doubt enabled and has prompted the Government to find new outlets for that increased revenue that they are receiving, and we have found applications made from various quarters as to how this surplus should be disposed of. It was well known at that time that Quebec was making urgent demands that they should be allowed some consideration in regard to their railways, on account of the amount they had expended upon certain roads, or should be relieved in some other manner. It was perfectly well known that if Quebec took a firm stand in a position of that kind, that they would be successful. I stated last year that I had no doubt that Quebec would be successful, but that if an increase of subsidy were granted to Quebec, Ontario must take the ground that she was entitled to an equivalent. The Dominion Government did relieve Quebec in two separate ways. In this case, out of a total of $7,172,000 given under this Act of 1884, Ontario is to get $2,882,289, and yet last year hon. gentlemen opposite held that we should not contend for this. But have they uttered one word of condemnation upon that other scheme that was carried through the Dominion Parliament last session, whereby Quebec got a return of $2,400,000 for aid granted to local railways, and Ontario was refused a single dollar for the same thing ? Have they found fault with that ? Was it not much better, Mr. Speaker that this Province should take the position that if Quebec should, get some more relief from the financial embarrassment under which she was labouring, it should be upon some basis whereby Ontario should receive an equivalent ? Hon. gentlemen opposite, I suppose, if they had occupied our position on this side of the House, would have refused this $2,800,000 and allowed Quebec to take her proportion. But I say, Mr. Speaker, that it is much better that we should press our claims when we see other provinces pressing theirs, and when we see that they are getting some advantages, endeavour to get an equivalent ourselves. I will, however, refer to the railway question later on.

I shall now give the House a statement of the expenditure for the past year. It has been as follows :

EXPENDITURE, 1884.

Civil Government...	$179,825 23
Legislation	141,440 28
Administration of Justice...	331,026 69
Education	531,651 00
Public Institutions—Maintenance	600,216 15
Immigration	43,369 92
Agriculture, Arts, etc.	195,362 64
Hospitals and Charities	94,218 83
Repairs and Maintenance, P.B.	70,149 91
Public Buildings	235,517 24
Public Works	27,717 40
Colonization Roads	185,772 55
Charges on Crown Lands	103,006 53
Miscellaneous	84,754 05
Refunds	46,006 70

Or a total expenditure under the Supply Bill of ...$2,870,035 12

Then there are certain classes of expenditure that are outside of the Supply Bill, for which we do not take an estimate. I will give them in detail.

Drainage Debentures	$ 71,998 04
Aid to Railways	253,783 41
Annuities	6,700 00
Municipal Loan Fund	150 00
Pensions to Widows	3,284 84
Drainage of Swamp Lands	1,600 00
Land Improvement Fund—Special..	338 26
	$337,854 55

Making the total expenditure under the Supply Bill and
     otherwise ....$ 3,207,889 67

Mr. MEREDITH.—At what rate are the Drainage Debentures issued?

Hon. Mr. ROSS.—These are all 5 per cent. Debentures.

Now, there are one or two items in this statement to which I may perhaps briefly refer. It will be noticed that our expenditure under Civil Government has very closely, I may say almost exactly, approximated what our estimate of expenditure was. We estimated $179,797, and we have expended $179,825. In Legislation it will be seen that there is a large over-expenditure; it is more particularly under the head of Sessional Clerks, Printing and

Stationery, Now these expenditures are yearly increasing. As I stated last year, it is an expenditure which is to a certain extent more under the control of the House than of the Government. As I pointed out before, when lengthy returns are applied for, no matter from which side of the House, the applications cannot be acceded to without the employment of considerable additional assistance in preparing and expense in printing them. We also find that there has been an increase last year in the cost of printing our ordinary departmental reports and other reports that are not purely departmental but which are for the information of the country. In 1884 we found that we had eight volumes of sessional papers. The largest number we have ever had before was six. Then I find that the cost of printing and distributing the reports alone,—annual reports and reports under the head of Agriculture, etc., amounted last year to $34,552. Well, now, all these reports are valuable. They contain information which is useful to the public. It would be impossible to withhold this information from the public, but at the same time it must be recognized that we cannot do this without involving considerable cost. In all the different branches under my own department, I have directed the attention of the officers to the necessity for the condensation of their reports, and in some cases that a lesser number should be distributed, but the House will itself have to a very large extent the control of the distribution, and I would invite the attention, co-operation and assistance of the Printing Committee of the House to this question, with a view of seeing whether this item can be reduced consistent with what is due to the country in the way of imparting useful information. I would not say that it is desirable that this information should be withheld from the country, even if the cost be large. Last year, after the Government had made provision for the distribution of the Agricultural College report, the value of which has been recognized time and again, the House itself took the matter in hand and asked for a further edition, as the public were looking eagerly for them, and that has been one reason why the expenditure under the head of Legislation has exceeded the estimate by the amount it has.

Then under the head of Administration of Justice, it will be seen that there has been something of an over-expenditure. That is mainly due to the amounts returned to counties. As explained before, the Criminal Justice expenditure is largely under the control of the municipalities, and the Government reimburse the municipalities a certain portion of that expenditure. Although in the previous year this had only amounted to $103,000, we took an estimate for $123,000, anticipating, as we had always found to be the case, that when times are hard crime is on the increase, yet we found in spite of our caculations that our estimate was too low, and instead of paying this $123,000, we have actually returned to the municipalities $132,081, or an over-expenditure of $8,281 that we have given to the municipalities in connection with Administration of Justice over and above what we had anticipated.

Then there has been an over-expenditure in the item of Immigration, and I may say, without going into details, which I suppose the Minister in charge will do hereafter, that a large part of that over-expenditure is for the carriage of immigrants in the previous year. The accounts had not been sent in by the railway authorities and therefore had not been paid that year, consequently our expenditures in 1884 were increased by this amount, which properly belonged to 1883.

Under Agriculture and Arts there is an over-expenditure, and I may state that the remark that I have already applied to Legislation applies here. About $8,000 has been for extra reports not charged to Legislation but charged under the head of Agriculture and Arts. I find that these reports amount to about $7,914. There was the butter-making report, $1,630; college report, $3,034; reports of the fruit-growers, entomological society, dairymen's association, forestry, $3,219, or a total of $7,914, which has been expended in regard to these agricultural reports, causing an over-expenditure of between $4,000 and $5,000.

Mr. MEREDITH.—You have not touched the over-expenditure of $14,000 for the Agricultural Farm?

Hon. Mr. Ross.—There is an over-expenditure in connection with the experimental farm. Last year we asked the House for a grant of $25,000 to purchase thorough-bred stock. It was impossible to tell exactly in an estimate of that kind what the cost would turn out to be. A great deal had to be left to the judgment of Professor Brown of the Agricultural College, under whose charge these purchases were made, and the expenditure in connection with the transportation of the stock and the retaining of them in quarantine for three months before they could be brought to the farm, under the regulations of the Dominion Government, made our expenditure, as will be seen by the public accounts, $27,000 instead of $25,000. Then, as I said, there is an expenditure of some $4,000 or $5,000 for reports, and the farm has cost somewhat more than we anticipated it would.

Then, under the head of Miscellaneous, it will be seen that there is a considerable over-expenditure. That is largely due to the expenditure imposed upon us in connection with the boundary dispute, an expenditure having been incurred of $29,327, when we only estimated an expenditure of some $10,000.

Mr. MEREDITH.—The hon. gentleman has passed over a large increase under Repairs and Maintenance of Departmental Buildings.

Hon. Mr. Ross.—Yes. It was a new account, a sort of experiment in character, whereby we placed Repairs, etc., under a separate account instead of having them charged under the departmental accounts, as formerly. It will be noticed that the over-expenditure has been largely in connection with the Parliament Buildings here and Government House. This subject has been referred to before, and it is hardly any use to mention it again now. A building such as this requires a very large expenditure for repairs to maintain it. Hon. gentlemen have the opportunity of seeing that for themselves, and I have no doubt will say that the repairs are not of that extravagant character which could be condemned.

There is also an over-expenditure in connection with the northerly and north-westerly parts of the province. That expenditure has been forced upon the Province partly by the unwarranted invasion of what was known as the disputed terri- tory, now disputed no longer. (Cheers.) An invasion instigated from what quarter it is not for me to say, but which threw upon the Government a largely increased expenditure in maintaining the authority of the Government in those parts. This over- expenditure has amounted to $6,703. It is not my place, Mr. Speaker, nor do I desire at the present time, in making this financial statement, to reflect upon the causes that led to this over-expendi- ture. That question can be discussed another time, and I do not wish to say anything that may be looked upon as of a hostile spirit. A part of that expenditure was also incurred on account of the turbulence that existed in consequence of the construction of the Canadian Pacific Railway in those parts, which caused an increase in expenditure which could neither be avoided nor foreseen.

I might refer very briefly to a large item of our expenditure, viz.: the maintenance of public institutions. Last year I gave the House tables shewing the comparative expenditure from year to year, and the deduction which I drew from those tables was that I believed that in regard to our Reformatories, the Central Prison, and the Institutions for the Deaf and Dumb and Blind, the Province had arrived at that position when the demands of that class of unfortunates had been overtaken. That although variations might take place from time to time, sometimes a little over and sometimes a little under the expenditure as at present, still we would not find in regard to these institutions that continuous and progressive increase that had existed in former years. That deduction was disputed by hon. gentlemen opposite. I am happy to say that from the returns given me by the Inspector of Prisons, which will appear in his report, another year's experience has added force to my contentions. I find in regard to these institutions (I am not re- ferring now to our Insane and Idiot Asylums) that the numbers that were confined and taken charge of in 1884 were less than in 1883, and these again, as I pointed out last year, were less than they had been in 1881 and 1882, or not increasing at any rate, so I think it may be assumed that in the cost of the maintenance of these unfortunate persons and criminals, we have arrived at the maximum expenditure, and any increases we may have in future years will be mainly due to the minor fluctuations that may take place from year to year, or to the increase of population.

I am sorry to say that in regard to our Lunatic and Idiot Asylums, these deductions do not hold good,—that we are still year by year finding a steady and progressive increase in the numbers admitted and in the cost of maintaining them, and this year, as will be seen by the estimates, the Government will find themselves obliged to ask an amount from the House for the purpose of providing additional accommodation for these classes. In connection with this matter I may refer very briefly to the fact that the Province of Ontario deals in the most liberal manner with these unfortunates. There is no other province or country that deals more liberally with them than we do (hear, hear). I have requested the Inspector of Prisons to make enquiries and give me the result as to what the practice is in regard to other institutions of a similar character in the United States and also in our own provinces, and from the returns he has given me, particulars of which will be given in his report, where hon. gentlemen will see them in detail, I find that in the United States there are seven States that assume the whole cost of the maintenance of their lunatics; I find that there are 18 in which the whole cost is thrown upon the municipalities from whence they come; and in 13 they divide the cost, a portion being paid by the State and a portion by the municipalities sending them. We in Ontario, because our revenue enabled us to do so, have maintained these lunatics at the whole cost of the province, and I think we have maintained them in a manner not only creditable to the people of the Province, but which has elicited the encomiums of those who are capable of judging, who have visited the institutions. It has been found that in no other Province or State are institutions conducted with more ability or efficiency than those in the Province

B

of Ontario.   I last year mentioned in regard to the cost that our
institutions were maintained at as low an average cost as any
others.   I think I may also say, speaking of the other Provinces
of the Dominion, that Quebec throws the cost of the maintenance
of lunatics upon the municipalities from whence they come.   In
Nova Scotia the Government only contribute $12,000 towards the
support of the asylum, which is placed under the charge of a com-
mission. They throw the whole of the rest of the expense, both
of the building and the maintenance, upon the municipalities from
whence the inmates come.

Now, in regard to over-expenditures.   There was a good
deal of over-expenditure last year, and I suppose it will
be one of the matters to which hon. gentlemen opposite will
take exception.   It is always likely that over-expenditure
will take place from time to time, and there is the more
likelihood that such will be the case in times of depression
than at any other time.   Hon. gentlemen will see that at Ottawa,
although they have an overflowing treasury, claiming a surplus
that they do not know what to do with, and therefore have no
inducement to under-estimate their expenditure, yet we find that
last year there have been very large and heavy over-expenditures
on the part of the Dominion.

Mr. WHITE.—That is no excuse for you.

Hon. Mr. Ross.—I do not claim that it is.   I am only pointing
out that in all expenditures under Government management, there
will be over-expenditures from time to time.   It is impossible for
a Government to foresee at the commencement of a year that
certain exigencies will arise which may call for an increase, and
these increases have to be met or the public interests will be
jeopardised.   The Government have to take the responsibility
when these over-expenditures arise, of meeting them, trusting to
the House to see that they have been justifiable.

I will now place before the House a statement of the financial
position of the Province as on the 31st December, 1884, as regards
assets and liabilities :

ASSETS OF THE PROVINCE.

1. Direct Investments :—

Dominion 6 per cent. Bonds	$500,000 00	
Market value over par value..........	50,000 00	
		$550,000 00
Drainage 5 per cent. Debentures, invested 31st December, 1884........	$241,602 48	
Tile Drainage 5 per cent. Debentures, invested 31st December, 1884....	26,239 61	
Overdue Interest on above.	1,649 90	
Drainage Works — Municipal Assessments	278,779 77	
		548,271 76
		$1,098,271 76

2. Capital Held and Debts Due by the Dominion to Ontario, Bearing Interest :—

U. C. Grammar School Fund, (2 Vict., Cap. 10)....	$312,769 04	
U. C. Building Fund, (18 Sect., Act 1854)	1,472,391 41	
Land Improvement Fund, (See Award).............	124,685 18	
Common School Fund, (Consol. Stats., Cap. 26)— proceeds realized to 1st July, 1867, $1,520,959.24 —after deducting Land Improvement Fund Portion belonging to Ontario	891,201 74	
Capital declared owing to the late Province of Canada by Dominion Act, (47 Vict., Cap. 4)— $5,397,503.13, bearing Interest at 5 per cent. Ontario's proportion on basis of Award as advised by Finance Department.................	2,848,289 52	
Ontario's Share of Library, (see Award)............	105,541 00	
		5,754,877 89

3. Other Debts Due to the Province :—

Balance *re* Municipal Loan Fund Debts............	$86,976 32	
" *re* Mortgages, Mechanics' Institute, Toronto, and Land at Orillia Asylum.........	7,905 08	
" *re* Mimico Lots...........................	6,527 58	
		101,408 98

4. Bank Balances :—

Current Accounts...............................	$196,507 22	
Special Deposits	71,579 75	
		268,086 97
Making a total of...........................		$7,222,645 60

Now, as regards the first item in the foregoing statement,— Dominion bonds—the premium that is taken into account ought to be the real market value of the security. The $500,000 of Dominion securities that we hold are not quoted in any stock list that I have seen. The Province of Ontario holds, I suppose, the whole of that issue which is now outstanding.

An Hon. MEMBER.—How long have they to run ?

Hon. Mr. Ross.—They do not mature till 1893, but I say that on looking at the stock lists I do not find that particular issue quoted in any of them, but I find that in the assets and liabilities of the Dominion there is a 6 per cent. issue amounting to some $500,000 still outstanding, and I presume that that is the one we hold, though the dates are not given, and I suppose that is the reason it is not quoted in the stock lists, because there are none on the market ; so in arriving at the market value I have taken the market value of other securities bearing the same rate of in- terest and falling due about the same time. From quotations from the same official authority before quoted, viz., the London *Econo- mist*, I find on the 3rd January there are quoted British Columbia securities bearing 6 per cent. falling due in 1894, just a year after ours, 110 to 112 ; I find New Brunswick 6 per cent. securities are quoted at 110. They are falling due two years before ours, and yet they are worth more than ours are valued at. Then I find Victoria debentures falling due in 1891, two years earlier than ours, are quoted at 109 to 112. And taking all these into con- sideration, not to exaggerate what would be the value of ours, I have placed the premium at the minimum of 10 per cent. upon their face value. Then we come to—

LIABILITIES OF THE PROVINCE AT PRESENT PAYABLE.

1. Balance due to Municipalities *re* Surplus Distribution..............	$2,000 45
2. Balance due to Municipalities, *re* Land Improvement Fund (balance of $124,685.18, see Award)...................................	3,608 55
3. *Quebec's share of Common School Fund made up as follows :—*	

Collections on account of Lands sold between 14th June, 1853, and 6th March, 1861 .... $838,557 52

Less 6 per cent. cost of Management $50,313 45

Less one-quarter for Land Improvement Fund........................... 209,639 38

259,952 83

$578,604 69

Collections on sales made since 6th March,
    1861................................... $302,657 68
  Less 6 per cent., cost of Management 18,159 46

                                                                   284,498 22

                                                        $863,102 91
Quebec's proportion according to population of 1881...............   357,370 21

        Total...................... .... $362,979 21

Leaving a surplus of assets after deducting liabilities presently payable. $6,859,666 39

(Loud applause and Opposition dissent.)

Now, hon. gentlemen opposite, I suppose, from the manner in which they have received this statement, will be inclined to dispute that we are entitled to claim this amount of $2,848,289 as part of our assets. I suppose that that is the ground that they will take, but I think when they come to read the statute under which that amount is given to Ontario, and to see the manner in which it is dealt with by the Finance Department at Ottawa, they will themselves come to the conclusion that it is clearly an asset of the Province which we have a right to take into account. I referred before to the Act of 1884, and declared that it was really an interpretation of the Act of 1873. I said that there was no other ground upon which the division which has been made could have been defended than the one that it is a carrying out of the Act of 1873. There is no ground upon which it could be given to Ontario and Quebec jointly unless in connection with the debt due by the late Province of Canada, because this interest was charged to the late Province of Canada in the Dominion accounts, and this is a return of that which had been charged to us and which had been deducted from the subsidies payable to the different provinces. Now let us read what the Act says is to be done : It says "the total amount of the half-yearly payments which would have been made on account of such increase from the 1st July, 1867, up to the 1st January, 1873, with interest on each at 5 per cent. per annum from the day on which it would have been so paid to the 1st day of July, 1884, shall be deemed *capital owing to the said provinces, respectively.*" (Hear, hear.) Now if this is capital owing to the provinces, it is a debt due to the provinces and it is clearly stated that it is capital owing to the provinces which is to be taken into account in the settlement of the accounts with the Dominion. Is it therefore not an asset to be taken into account ?

Mr. MEREDITH.—I would ask the hon. gentleman if it is not another invasion of Provincial rights ?

Hon. Mr. ROSS.—No, it is an acknowledgment of Provincial rights. The Act distinctly says that it is capital owing to the provinces, and they have made the division, as I stated before, upon the basis of the award, while they have given an equivalent to Manitoba, British Columbia and Prince Edward Island upon the basis of population, clearly recognizing that it is merely carrying out what was the intention of the Act of 1873, and a matter to be settled and taken into account between the Province and the Dominion in the settlement of their accounts. Then how does the Finance Department at Ottawa treat it ? If it is not capital owing to us, if we are only entitled to the interest as part of our annual subsidy, surely we have no right to have the principal credited to us in the accounts of the Dominion, yet we find in the Public Accounts of 1884, that it is entered to our credit. The Province is directly credited with it, and its liability on account of the debt of the old province is reduced by that amount. Are we, therefore, not entitled to claim it as an asset now ? In none of the former Acts providing for increases to Nova Scotia or New Brunswick are the words used " capital owing." In all these other cases they treat it as and call it an increase of subsidy, but in this case it is treated as " capital owing " and is credited to the respective provinces. I have no knowledge of what was in the minds of those who framed the Act, but I think I can see why it was placed in that way. Some of the provinces are indebted to the Dominion, and by making this capital owing and applying the amounts placed in the Act to the credit of their respective accounts the Dominion collects the balances owing.

Mr. MEREDITH.—Why don't you get a cheque for the amount granted Ontario ?

Hon. Mr. Ross.—We don't want it; it is invested there, drawing five per cent interest. We cannot make a better investment.

I say, therefore, Mr. Speaker, that by the action of the Finance Department at Ottawa themselves, they have treated it as a payment to the Provinces to which they are entitled to credit in the settlement of accounts; and, I say again, that if any of the Provinces who had overdrawn their accounts with the Dominion are entitled to have these amounts placed to their credit as a set-off against their over-drafts, we, who have not overdrawn, are as clearly entitled to take credit for this $2,800,000 as an asset of this Province.

Then, also. in the statement of assets and liabilities given by the Dominion in the Public Accounts of 1884, hon. gentlemen will find in the statement as given there, which includes the balances due by the Provinces to the Dominion, which they take into account as an asset in 1883 and 1884, that the amounts of these debts are decreased by the amounts which these Provinces are credited with. Are we, then, not clearly entitled to treat it as an increase of *our* assets? Most assuredly we are; there can be no question about that.

It is but right, however, to say to the House that there are, in addition to the liabilities I have named, other liabilities of the Province. I do not dispute that, but I have made a distinction in deducting the liabilities from the assets. I have deducted those liabilities that are at present payable. All the liabilities which I have named here are liabilities which we may be called upon to-morrow to pay. There are other liabilities which were never intended to be considered as present liabilities. In regard to the old railway certificates, the Government took the ground that they could not, out of the present revenue, undertake to pay the amount of the two or three or four thousand dollars a mile granted to these railways at the time, but they said, " We will give you, in the future, certain amounts, yearly or half-yearly, in aid of the construction of your railways," and the certificates were issued for the convenience of these railways, for the purpose of enabling them to raise money upon them if they so desired, but they were always intended to represent a future liability, to be paid out of revenue of the year in which they fell due. Now, that position has been disputed by hon. gentlemen opposite; I suppose it will be disputed yet; but I think you will find an exactly similar liability on the part of the Dominion, which, Mr. Courtney, the Deputy Finance Minister, treats exactly in the same way. In looking over the introductory remarks in the Dominion Accounts of 1884, it will be found that Mr. Courtney refers to the increased liability made during the year in connection with railway subsidies. He says, " In addition to the liabilities referred to, the several Provinces forming the Dominion were credited in their debt account with $7,172,297, and liabilities were incurred as subsidies to the various railways under the Act 47, Vic. chap. 8, amounting to $6,176,400, which amount does not include the two sums of $170,000 and $30,000 per annum for fifteen years."

Now here, by the way, is another evidence in addition to what I have already adduced, in support of our being entitled to claim this $2,800,000 as an asset, when Mr. Courtney treats the total capital as a liability of the Dominion. If it is a liability there, it is an asset here. The Dominion Government in granting railway subsidies, granted, as we did, direct payments to some of them, but, in the case of two of them, they took the course taken by this Legislature in former years, and agreed only to give to one road $170,000 a year, and to another $30,000 a year, but Mr. Courtney does not treat this as a present liability. He expressly says that he does not include them. Now, I say that this shows that according to Dominion practice these are not to be treated as a present liability, but a liability of the future.

Then, we have the liability on account of annuities issued last year. They are not a present liability, either; they cannot be demanded at the present time, but it is a liability falling due in the future, and if we were merely a commercial corporation, a banking or loan society, we would be entitled to take these yearly liabilities and capitalize them against ourselves. That would be one mode of doing it, and if we were to take that course and follow that pursued by such institutions as I have named, we could shew a far better record than I have shewn, because if we were on the one side to shew the capitalization of our liabilities, we should be equally entitled to capitalize these yearly sums which are guaranteed to us, and of which we are in receipt as guaranteed revenue. We would be entitled to capitalize the sums received from the Dominion Government as subsidy. Now, what would that amount to? We would be entitled to claim, as the present value of these subsidies, $23,000,000. But we do not do so. In all financial statements, whether government, municipal, or of financial institutions, the system of book-keeping prevails which is applicable to their several requirements. The same systems cannot be adopted, and the same statements cannot be given. I say, in the case of a commercial or loan company they would also take into account, as part of their capital, the buildings they own, the land they own, the debts due upon the land, etc. Now, we might upon that basis take into account all the unsold real estate belonging to the Province, all the public buildings which have been erected. Formerly the Dominion Government did count among their assets the value of all their buildings erected, but of late years they have discontinued it. We might also claim the unpaid balances upon crown lands, but we do not do so. But there is one point to which I might refer, as shewing that annual liabilities of that kind are not taken into account by the Dominion Government. Some years ago, at the time the Washington Treaty was negotiated, certain timber duties that formerly had been collected by the Province of New Brunswick, were abolished and given up as part of the equivalent that was given by Canada in that settlement. The Province of New Brunswick applied to the Dominion

Government for the reimbursement of the amount. The Dominion Government voted New Brunswick an annual payment of $150,000 in perpetuity in lieu of these timber duties. Have they ever capitalized that and treated it as a liability? But I wish to guard myself in this way. I consider these annuities and these railway certificates as liabilities, but I do not give them in the statement I have given now, because I have only given the liabilities which are at present payable, which we might be called upon to make good to-morrow. If we were to come to a settlement with Quebec at once, that Province might demand their proportion of the Common School Fund, and we would be obliged to make it good. But those which are payable out of annual revenue we do not take into account in this statement of liabilities that we may say are presently payable. They are liabilities, however, which are payable in the future.

Now it has been the practice for some years in these discussions upon the Financial Statement, in fact, the general course of criticism has been upon the other side of the House, to draw comparisons of the expenditure now and the expenditure under Sandfield Macdonald. I think, Mr. Speaker, that it is about time that these comparisons should cease. I trust that hon. gentlemen on the opposite side of the House have become tired of them. The hon. member for West Toronto stated last year that these comparisons were useless—there was no doubt they were. Do you suppose that you could shew extravagance against the Government of the present time by comparing the expenditure of the Province of Ontario now with what it was in 1871? It would be futile and useless, and I do not propose to make any such comparison. But hon. gentlemen have also drawn attention frequently to the surplus that was, as it were, bequeathed by the Sandfield Macdonald Government to Mr. Mowat, claiming that while he handed over securities to a large amount that were available at that time, we have reduced that surplus to a large extent, or at least have not accumulated surplus as rapidly as he. We do not mean to say that we have accumulated a surplus of a million

or a million and a half year by year, as they say Sandfield Macdonald did ; but I think it is nothing but right to look at the
bequest made us by Sandfield, and see what has been done with
it. It has been claimed that Mr. Mowat has not accumulated a surplus equal to what he did. Mr. Mowat has never
recognized it as being the sole aim of a Government to raise
a surplus. His pride and glory has been, not to accumulate
a surplus, but rather to expend the money in the interests
of the people, as far as possible relieving local burdens, and
meeting the legitimate demands of a growing Province. Now
in 1872, Sandfield handed over to the succeeding Government
in investments and bank balances $3,810,964, and if we
add to that what was found to be the collectable balance
due by municipalities under the Municipal Loan Fund, viz.,
$1,273,840, we find there was handed over $5,084,804, less what
was then Quebec's proportion of the Common School Fund
that had been collected up to that time, $105,800, or a total of
investments and debts due to the Province at that time of
$4,979,004. In this, I may say, I am not taking into account the
Dominion Trust Funds, which I will leave out of the account in
this comparison. Now what was done with that $4,900,000 ? The
very first act of Mr. Mowat was to distribute to the people, in
direct payments to the municipalities, $3,388,068.

Mr. MEREDITH.—How much of that did you get back under
the Tilley Act ?

Hon. Mr. ROSS.—We did not get back any of that. By the
Tilley Act we only got relief to the extent of the interest on the
debt assumed. We have got that now, but I am not going to
take that into account in making this comparison, because that is
one of the funds in the hands of the Dominion. I thought the
hon. gentleman disputed that we are entitled to this $2,800,000 ;
but now he wants to charge us with this sum. But I say that
there was handed over to Mr. Mowat in investments, etc.,
$4,979,004, and his very first act was to distribute $3,388,068.
His next was to give in aid to local railways, $3,911,880. In

these two sums alone he gave back to the people $7,299,948, or $2,320,944 more than he had received altogether from Sandfield Macdonald. (Hear, hear.) Now, I would ask hon. gentlemen if the people were not better satisfied with this disposition of the Sandfield Macdonald surplus than if we had retained it and were able to show them a larger surplus now? The people have already, on more than one occasion, expressed themselves, and I am satisfied that they will say that it is far better that Mr. Mowat should have relieved local burdens, far better that he should have aided these local railways than have kept these funds and hoarded them up in the provincial treasury in order to be able to say that we have got a very large surplus at the present time.

I might say this, that there are only three items of our governmental expenditure that are absolutely necessary to be undertaken by a Government, viz., Civil Government, Administration of Justice, and Legislation; all the rest might be handed over to the municipalities, and could be provided for by them if the Government were disposed to throw the onus upon them. If the receipts of the Province were so restricted, they might refuse grants to Education, Agriculture and Arts, Administration of Justice in counties, Hospitals and Charities, and all these are now branches of governmental expenditure. The Government might either reduce these grants or relieve themselves of them altogether and throw them upon the municipalities, if their whole purpose and aim were to accumulate a surplus. If such had been the policy of Mr. Mowat, he would have been able, by that means, to have shewn to-day a surplus of twenty or twenty-five millions, and yet the whole argument of hon. gentlemen opposite is directed particularly in that line, as if because our expenditure now is increased, because our actual bank balance is reduced, that therefore there has been extravagance on the part of Mr. Mowat, whereas we claim it as our greatest glory that we have, so far as our provincial revenue will allow, met all reasonable demands, and still have a nice little nest egg in the provincial treasury. (Applause.)

Now, in regard to these particular branches of expenditure which I say might be considered to be purely local if the Government were disposed to throw the burden of them upon the municipalities, Mr. Mowat has paid for education, $6,598,251 ; we have paid for the maintenance of public institutions, in supporting the insane and idiots, as well as criminals, $5,759,416 ; in aid to agriculture and arts we have distributed $1,423,315 ; to hospitals and charities, $858,366 ; in aid to counties towards payment of the expenses of local administration of justice, $1,649,-150 ; in colonization roads, which might also be claimed to be a burden which might be thrown upon the localities, $1,393,481, or a total in these branches named of $17,681,979. (Hear, hear.) I have not included public buildings and works, because they are of a mixed character, although there is a large portion of it which might be classed in the same way. In regard to the maintenance of criminals and lunatics, we know very well that for many years our gaols were crowded with lunatics who were maintained there at the expense of the counties. We know that in many cases these unfortunates were maintained at the expense of their own families. All these have been relieved now, and I am happy to say that on the 31st December we had overtaken all reasonable demands applied for from the gaols, although we must provide increased accommodation required for the coming year.

Now, perhaps it would be as well to see how these grants to these different branches have been increased since 1871. I say that Mr. Mowat, if he had kept in view as the main object of his government the accumulation of a surplus, might have said, " we won't increase the grants to these institutions beyond what they were in 1871." That would have satisfied hon. gentlemen opposite ; that is what they say we should have done. But we have increased the grants and are expending more just because it is necessary that we should do so ; because the people want it ; because it is relieving local burdens to do so. Take education; in 1871 Sandfield Macdonald gave in grants to education, $351,-306 ; if this payment had been continued at the same rate for the thirteen years since that time, the total amount which would have been paid would have been $4,566,978. Mr. Mowat has actually given in grants to education $6,598,251, or, he has given back to the people in the shape of increased grants to schools $2,031,273 more than if he had continued them on the same scale as in Sandfield's time. I think that is a very fair way of putting it, to simply meet the objection of hon. gentlemen opposite, who point to an increased expenditure, and endeavour to draw from that that there has been extravagance on the part of the Government. Then in regard to agriculture and arts ; Sandfield gave in 1871, $76,381. If you take thirteen years at that expenditure it would be equal to $992,953. Mr. Mowat has given in aid to agriculture and arts, $1,423,315, or $430,362 more than if he had continued the grants on the same scale as in 1871. Then as to hospitals and charities, Sandfield's expenditure in 1871 was $40,260, which for thirteen years would amount to $523,380, whereas Mr. Mowat has given in grants to hospitals and charities during these thirteen years $858,366, or an increase of $334,-986 more than if he had continued on the same scale as Sandfield Macdonald. In Public Institutions maintenance, Sandfield only expended in 1871 $171,423. Now, in relieving the municipalities from the burden of maintaining these unfortunates Mr. Mowat has in these thirteen years actually expended $5,759,416, or $3,430,917 more than if he had kept the expenditure down to Sandfield's figures. (Hear, hear.) Then, in regard to administration of justice, taking the same years, Sandfield Macdonald expended $104,049, (and recollect, as I said before, when I am taking administration of justice, I am only taking that part of it which is money directly refunded to the municipalities), so that in thirteen years we would have given, had we continued in the same way, $1,352,637 whereas Mr. Mowat has given back to the municipalities $1,649,150, or $296,513 more than if he had followed the same scale as Sandfield. In colonization roads Sandfield gave $55,419 in 1871; thirteen years at that rate would give $720,317, whereas the actual amount we have given to the inhabitants of these outlying districts in con-

structing roads, which are certainly of great benefit to the
country, has been $1,393,481, or $673,164 more than if we had
continued the expenditure merely on the scale left by Sandfield
Macdonald. Now these branches of expenditure, which I say are
purely to relieve the municipalities, are not expenditures from
which the government derive any benefit. As I said before, if
their aim was to accumulate a surplus, they might have thrown
the whole of them upon the municipalities, or have continued
them merely on the old scale, but instead of following that course,
Mr. Mowat has, with a liberality which is approved of by the
people, increased the grants and has given back to the municipalities in thirteen years $7,197,215 more than if he had con-
tinued these payments merely on the scale of 1871.

Mr. CARNEGIE—Does the hon. gentleman apply the same rule
to receipts?

Hon. Mr. ROSS—Yes; I have no hesitation in doing so.
I took up the question of receipts last year, and if the hon.
gentleman will refer to the statement I made then, he will see, I
think, that I gave a table of what were the receipts of the
Province under Sandfield Macdonald, and every year since, and
I showed that we had only been receiving an excess of $60,000 a
year more than Sandfield Macdonald. (Cheers.) I challenge the
hon. gentleman to say if that is not correct; he has the statement
now in his hands, and he will find there that the amount we
have received over and above the revenue which Sandfield Macdonald received was only about $60,000. And I might also say
this, and I am glad the hon. gentleman has given me the opportunity, that we have given back to the people more than that
$60,000 in remission of revenue. By the abolition of taxes in
Division and County Courts we have given back to the people
some $30,000 a year, and in reduction of marriage licenses we
have given back to the people another $30,000, so that we would
have had $60,000 of additional revenue had we not reduced it
for the people's benefit in the way I have pointed out. The hon.
gentleman will find all this information in my last year's financial
statement, which contains a table of receipts from 1873 onwards.

Now, I suppose the House will be anxious to know what progress has been made in the settlement of the disputed accounts with the Dominion. I am sorry to say that the progress has not been what I hoped for and anticipated. It will be in the knowledge of hon. gentlemen that it would have been impossible to have secured a meeting of the Provincial Treasurers and the Finance Minister until the meetings of both the Provincial Legislatures and the Dominion House had been brought to a close. The meeting of the Quebec Legislature did not close until June, so that it was impossible to secure a meeting until that time. When that did close, it was found that Sir Leonard Tilley's absence in England would prevent any meeting for the settlement of these accounts. He did not return until September and immediately I applied to him for the purpose of arranging a conference whereby we might arrive at some conclusion and make some progress towards the settlement. A meeting was arranged for, to take place on the 21st October of last year. The Treasurer of Quebec and myself met Sir Leonard Tilley on that occasion, but as the main items of dispute were matters which involved legal contentions, principally respecting the charges made in regard to Indian annuities, Sir Leonard objected in the absence of Sir John Macdonald to take them up, as they were matters pertaining to Sir John's own department, and we therefore failed to make any progress in regard to the main items at issue on that occasion. Then there was another item we ought to have had settled on that occasion, a claim which we had in connection wih the Land Improvement Fund; the Treasurer of Quebec objected to go into that, because he said that before he discussed it he wanted to have the opinion and advice of his Attorney-General, as it was a legal question and might turn largely upon legal issues. You will see therefore that in two of the most important points which we had met to discuss, we were baulked; but I may say that some progress was made, and, when we come to look at the result, rather material progress. We arranged at that time that Mr. Courtney should make a recast of the accounts in consequence of the credit of interest which has been given us under the Dominion Act of 1884. It was also arranged that the Indian claims, as these might involve legal points, should be placed in a suspense account, so that any delays that might occur in regard to those need not interfere with a settlement of the other matters. That recast of the accounts, although pressed for very strongly, has not yet been received by us, and the excuse offered, which is perhaps a reasonable one, is that Mr. Courtney has been so engaged in preparations for the meeting of the House, etc., that he has not had the time to give attention to it. But there was one matter which was decided at this meeting which is a matter of importance to the Province. You will recollect that last year, in drawing attention to these Indian claims, I objected to the sum that was charged to the accounts of the Dominion with the Provinces, of $303,280, charged to us as at date of 1867, as capitalization of Indian annuities payable under the Robinson Treaty, and that I said that this capitalization was altogether erroneous. A return will be submitted of correspondence which took place, from which it will be seen that in June last, I drew attention to what appeared to me a grave error in that calculation. I had previously got a statement from Mr. Courtney of the basis upon which the calculation was made, and I found, as I had anticipated, that they had capitalized these annuities twice over. As I mentioned last year, in the statement of debt that was submitted at the time of confederation in 1867, there was $88,000 charged as capitalization of annuities. That was the capitalization of Indian annuities then payable under the Robinson Treaty, viz., $4,400 annually. This $303,280, which they charged again, was the capitalization of the $4 per head claimed as the total annuity payable to the Indians, and thus included this $88,000 again. I pointed this out to Mr. Courtney and Sir Leonard Tilley at our meeting. The matter was discussed, and it was admitted that an error had been made in that amount, and that they had charged us more than they were entitled to by $88,000, and charged us this as at date of 1867, so that it makes it now, calculating interest up to the present time, a credit of $208,842. That was one

C

matter settled on that occasion in favour of the united provinces.
Now I may say that the Act passed by the Dominion last
session, has paved the way for a more speedy settlement of the
accounts. The Dominion Government having not only assumed
the whole of the debt up to 1873, but also relieved the Provinces
from the interest formerly charged upon it, we have not the same
interest in closely scrutinizing the items composing it. The differ-
ences between the Provinces and the Dominion, in regard to the
accounts submitted are, I may say, now practically reduced to
three main items : first, the Indian claims, then the Land Improvement Fund, and then the interest allowed us on the Building
Fund. The Indian claims, as I mentioned last year, are made up
as follows : in the first place, they charge us $140,000 for arrears
of payments to Indians under the Robinson Treaty as at date of
1867 ; and then, as I have already mentioned, they charge us
capitalization of annuities, $303,280, as at the same date. On
getting a statement from the Indian Department as to how these
arrears were made up, I found that they had allowed to the
Indians the increased allowance provided for by the Robinson
Treaty of $4 per head, actually from the date the Treaty
had gone into operation, 1850, although for years after not a
single dollar had been received as revenue from the territory.
The treaty provided that a certain fixed sum of $4,400 should
be paid to the Indians annually, with a provision that if in future
years the revenue derived from the territory should enable the
Province to do so without loss, these annuities might be increased
to a sum not exceeding $4 per head. Well, it is clear that until
the revenue from the territory does enable the Province to do so
without loss, the Indians are not entitled to this $4 per head.

Mr. MEREDITH.—Did the Provincial authorities assent to this
increase ?

Hon. Mr. ROSS.—No, never. These arrears are charged as at
date of 1867, as arrears at Confederation due to the Indians. I
suppose what the hon. gentleman is referring to is a despatch
sent by the Hon. the Attorney-General in 1874, seven years after

Confederation had been in operation, and therefore has no connection with these arrears.

Mr. MEREDITH.—It assented to the increase.

Hon. Mr. Ross.—Only partially. It did not assent that they should be charged to the Province, and it had no reference to the arrears. I am only dealing now with the item of $140,000 charged as arrears. They charge that as due to the Indians, that is the $4 per head from the time the Treaty went into operation, although, as I say, for some years thereafter there was not a dollar of revenue received from the territory. Then I may say that up to Confederation, taking into account the receipts derived from the territory both from sales of lands, timber dues, and mining licenses, and taking into account also the payments that had been made to the Indians, the disbursements in surveys and construction of roads, the whole receipts of the territory fell short of what had been disbursed by over $250,000, so that there was no ground for giving any increase up to that date, because we had never had a revenue sufficient to meet the expenditure.

Mr. MEREDITH.—That was in the discretion of the old Parliament of Canada.

Hon. Mr. Ross.—But the old Parliament never exercised the discretion. The Indians were never paid it to this day. This charge against the Province now is a thing of recent discovery. The Indians never claimed it until 1873, and yet as at date of 1867 we are charged with $140,000 and interest from that time. I say there is not a shadow of foundation for that charge, and it must be wiped out of the accounts altogether. That sum, with interest, amounts $332,249, which we are entitled to have credit for. Then there is the claim for capitalization, $303,280. I have already said that they acknowledge an error in that of $88,000 ; but the $303,280, which is based upon the increased annuity of $4, is capitalized as at date of 1867, and interest charged the Province upon it since that date ; but if we are liable at all, we were not liable at that date. Up to Confederation the disbursements had exceeded the receipts by $250,000, as I explained before, and it was not till the year 1872 that the receipts from the territory balanced the expenditure that had been incurred, even in our own Province and through our own Crown Lands Department, so that, taking these expenditures by Ontario alone, it could not be until 1872 that there was any shadow of a ground for making that claim. But there is this to be taken into consideration, it is a bargain not between the Province of Ontario and the Indians, it is a contract between the Crown and the Indians, and the Crown is represented by all the Governments in Canada, either by the Government of the old Province of Upper and Lower Canada, or by the Dominion, or by the Province of Ontario. It is a contract between the Crown and the Indians, and whatever expenditure has been incurred by any one of these Governments necessary for the opening up of the country, or which has been the means of increasing the revenue that has been derived from it by increasing the value of the land, must be taken into account, before it could be said that the Province or the Crown could give the increased payment without incurring loss. We must know what that expenditure is before we can say when the Indians would be entitled to the increase. Again, the Indians never claimed it until 1873, and it was never recognized by the Crown until 1875. We claim, therefore, that if we were liable at all, and if the surplus of revenue would warrant it, that liability only commenced when it was recognized by the Crown. We claim further, however ; we claim that we are not liable at all, because at the time of Confederation, as I have already stated, the Dominion capitalized these annuities payable under these treaties in the sum of $88,000 and charged them as part of the debt of the Province, and I claim, therefore, that there was a settlement virtually of the whole liability under the treaty. The Dominion assumed the $88,000 and agreed to pay the annuities. The treaty provided for both a possible increase on decrease of the annuities. It provided that the increased rate might be paid, provided the revenues from the territory exceeded the expenditures to such an extent as to warrant the increase. It also provided that if the Indian population decreased to the extent of two-thirds of what it was at the time it was executed, the annuities to the Indians should be decreased in proportion ; therefore there was a liability which the Dominion Government had assumed to the amount of $88,000 which was liable to either increase or decrease. Suppose the Indian population had become extinguished, would the Dominion Government have paid us back any of that $88,000 they capitalized then ? Not a bit of it. They took that on speculation, as it were, and if there is any increase to be given by the Crown, the Dominion Government are liable for it ; they agreed to pay the liability under the treaty. Then there is another ground for objection ; the treaties provided for a decrease but not for an increase in population ; but I find by the return that has been sent to us that they are paying them $4 per head upon a largely increased Indian population. Indians who never came forward to claim compensation under the treaty are coming forward now and claiming it, so that we have strong grounds to claim that the capitalization charge of $303,280 is erroneous altogether, or, if it is a liability upon us to any amount, it is one of a very much smaller extent than charged.

I now desire to refer to the Land Improvement Fund. In our contention for the Land Improvement Fund we are not contending for a matter in which the Province as a province has any direct interest ; it would rather be against the Provincial Treasury ; but we are contending in this as the representatives of the municipalities to whom the fund is due. This matter has been discussed before, but as many hon. members were not in the House when these discussions took place, and I know from the correspondence that I have received from many municipalities that it is a matter that they are greatly interested in, so that all the information which can be given I am satisfied will be of the greatest interest to the municipalities, I will perhaps refer to it more fully than I otherwise would. The Land Improvement Fund was established by 16 Vic., chap. 39. By that Act one-quarter of the proceeds of sales of Common School lands were set apart for local improvements in the localities where the lands

sold were situate. By the same Act one-fifth of the sales of
Crown Lands were set apart for the same purpose. In 1861, by
Order in Council, this fund was put an end to so far as future
sales were concerned, but the before-mentioned proportions of
collections on sales made between 1853 and 1861 were still to be
credited to this fund. Statements submitted by the Dominion
at the arbitration between Ontario and Quebec, showed that the
one-quarter of the School Lands so collected amounted to $124,-
685.18, and the one-fifth of similar collections from Crown Lands
to $101,171. By the award the Land Improvement Fund was
declared to be an asset of the Province of Ontario, but did not
state what the amount of that fund was. Whatever it was it
belonged to Ontario. The arbitrators having decided that Quebec
was entitled to share in the proceeds of the Common School
Lands, it was necessary that they should take into account the
claim that Ontario had for Land Improvement Fund in those
lands, and they directed that before making the division between
Ontario and Quebec the sum of $124,685.18 should be deducted
from the Common School Fund and credited to the Land Improvement Fund, and it was only in this way that any direct
reference was made to the $124,685. They made no special
reference to the $101,171; they were not called upon to do so.
They simply declared that the Land Improvement Fund was to
be an asset of Ontario, without declaring what that fund was or
what it consisted of, further than that the $124,685 was to be a
portion of it. Those who made out the Dominion accounts had
evidently been misled into supposing that this $124,685 was the
whole amount of the fund, and had overlooked the amount
accrued from Crown Lands. But the same principles govern
both. They were both provided for by the same Act, and the
one is as much a liability of the late Province of Canada as the
other, but the fact that the $101,171 is not specifically given in
the award may have led the Province of Quebec to dispute this
item. At the meeting in October the Treasurer of Quebec refused
to assent to that sum being placed to the credit of Ontario until

he should have an opportunity of discussing the matter with his Attorney-General. The item is therefore still unsettled. But I have not the shadow of a doubt that when it comes to be discussed, Ontario will be able to maintain its claims on behalf of the municipalities to this $101,171. (Hear, hear.)

These are not the only claims, however, which are in dispute We find that we are confronted with new claims in regard to Indian payments—claims which I am satisfied that the House and the country have never heard of before. We are confronted with a claim of $68,702, claimed to be due the Mississaguas of the Credit under a treaty executed in 1820,—a claim which they themselves never preferred, and was never recognized by the old Province of Upper Canada, under whose jurisdiction and government these lands were, and with whom the treaty was made; a claim that was never recognized by the old Province of Canada after the union, a claim that has not been presented by the Dominion to the Province of Ontario for seventeen years since Confederation. In fact, for upwards of sixty years this claim has remained in abeyance, and now we are presented with a claim of $16,838, principal, and $51,834, interest, payable to these Indians. Well, I think it is rather extraordinary that we have not heard of this claim before, and then, I may say that it was only presented to us a few days before the meeting at Ottawa in October last. It seems to be a new discovery. But what will surprise the House more is that but a few days before that meeting took place, on the 21st October, we found that an Order in Council had been passed by the Dominion Government on the 7th of that month, on the recommendation of Sir John Macdonald, directing that this sum should be charged against the Province as a liability and credited to the Indian Fund; and more, he directed that the Indians should be notified that the amount had been placed to their credit, and they have actually been allowed to draw a portion of the money. I say, sir, that this action is most astonishing, particularly when we consider that an arrangement was entered into between the Dominion and the Province some years ago that no charge should be made by the Dominion or allowed against the Provinces without the concurrence of the Provincial Treasurers, yet in defiance of that we find this charge made against the Province ; and to complicate matters and enhance the difficulties of a settlement, we find the Indians have been notified that the amount is placed to their credit, and that they have drawn some $6,000.

Mr. MEREDITH.—If it is not a valid claim, it won't hurt you very much.

Hon. MR. ROSS.—But the hon. gentleman can see that there may be a difficulty after the lapse of sixty years in legally proving whether it is or is not a valid claim. Even if the Provinces were not able clearly to prove that the claim was invalid, the long time which has been allowed to elapse would point to its being a fair subject for compromise. But the House can see how much the difficulty of arriving at a fair settlement has been aggravated by notifying the Indians that the amount is at their credit. I say it was a precipitation altogether unnecessary on the part of the Dominion Government. When it had been as long in abeyance as sixty-four years, there was no urgency for a few days until the Provinces had been notified. I say it was a most extraordinary proceeding, and certainly requires some explanation.

Then we have got another new claim on behalf of the Chippewas of Lakes Simcoe and Huron, $196,000 arrears and $125,000 capitalization, for lands which these Indians claim belonged to them, but were ceded by the Ojibbeways under the Robinson Treaty to the Crown, these Indians claiming that the Ojibbeways had no right to cede them because they never belonged to them, and that they, who never were parties to the treaty at all, are to receive the same annuity as given to the Ojibbeways, viz., $4 per head, and that to date back to the year 1850, making $196,000 for arrears and the $125,000 for capitalization of future annuities. It strikes me, though I am not a lawyer, and do not pretend to give any legal opinion upon the question, that if the Ojibbeways pretend to cede lands which did not belong to them, and if the

Crown agreed to pay $4 a head for lands which the tribe claimed the right to cede ; if it turns out they did not own the land, the Crown is not bound to pay. If liable to one we cannot be liable to the other. We cannot pay two tribes of Indians for the same land. We agreed to pay $4 a head to certain Indians for the land they claimed to own, and if it turns out that the lands did not belong to them, the Crown is not liable for the annuity promised.

It appears there have been negotiations going on with these Indians for some years in regard to this claim, principally during 1883 and 1884, and we find now this claim charged against the Province. I cannot conceive that it is put forward with any degree of sincerity, but merely trumped up for the purpose of making it appear that Ontario has greater liabilities than is admitted.

But then I may say that we have some claims against the Dominion also, and I believe we are justly entitled to the amount they represent. In the first place, by the unanimous decision of the Supreme Court, two years ago, in the Queen v. Robinson, the Supreme Court declared that all the inland fisheries were under the control of the Provinces and not of the Dominion ; that the Dominion had no control over them and no right to collect licenses ; that the right to fish was vested in the owners of the land. The effect of that is that the Dominion Government have been collecting, in Ontario and other Provinces, revenues for fishing licenses to which they had no right. We have, therefore, a clear claim to the return of revenues derived from that source. I have taken the Dominion accounts, and find that there was since Confederation $89,249 collected in Ontario, which, with interest at five per cent., as they have charged us, compounded, would amount now to $129,425.

Mr. MEREDITH.—What kind of fisheries are these ?

Hon. MR. ROSS.—The classification of fisheries in the Dominion accounts covers all inland fisheries.

Mr. MEREDITH.—It covers all lake fisheries ?

Hon. MR. ROSS.—Certainly.

Then we have another charge to make against the Dominion Government, but of the amount of which unfortunately the House and Province are ignorant. I refer to the revenues they have been collecting from what was lately known as the Disputed Territory, now, I trust, disputed no longer. The Dominion Government have been collecting large revenues from lands, timber limits and minerals, and when we are able to get at the particulars, we shall have a large claim against the Dominion for these revenues, unless we find, as perhaps there is too much reason to fear, that they have been sacrificed by the Dominion Government, by grants to political favourites, without valuable consideration.

Then we have a third claim against the Dominion Government, but a claim that cannot, I suppose, be legally enforced as I think the other two can, but a claim that is equitable and a claim which in all justice Ontario is entitled to press.

Mr. MEREDITH.—Consequential damages ?

Hon. Mr. Ross.—Not consequential damages, but a claim that ought to be conceded if we are treated the same as other Provinces. I refer to the reimbursement of aid granted to Provincial railways, seized by the Dominion, in the same manner as it was given to the Province of Quebec by the legislation of last session. The House will be aware that the Province of Quebec obtained at that time $2,396,000 as a return of aid given to local roads. It is not for me to say whether the policy pursued by the Dominion under that Act was a wise one or not. It is not for me to refer to the extraordinary pressure reported to have been brought to bear upon the Dominion Government to compel them to give countenance to the claim made by that Province. I do not wish to refer to that here. My duty, as the financial officer of the Province, is to watch the manner in which the other Provinces are dealt with, and see that the Province I represent receives equal justice with them. The past attitude of the Dominion Government in regard to Dominion railways was this, that they recognized their liability only as regards large inter-national lines, such as the Inter-colonial and the Canada Pacific ; they recognized no liabilily as regards local lines wholly within the Provinces. To the Provinces heretofore had been left the recognition of the demands for local railways. These demands have been liberally met by the Provinces. The charters for these local roads had been obtained from the Provincial Parliaments. These charters gave them privileges and imposed conditions upon which the aid was granted. These roads were under the control of the Provincial Parliaments, the conditions could be altered, waived, or new conditions imposed at the will of the people under whose charter they existed. By their charters conditions were imposed as to the carriage of agricultural products, lumber and wood, making indeed a tariff, as it were, for these railways, and under the conditions imposed was the aid only extended. In 1882 these regulations between the roads and the local Parliaments were, by one enactment of the Dominion, swept away and blotted out, and the local control of the roads taken from the people who had built them.

Mr. MEREDITH.—Does the hon. gentleman contend that the effect of the Dominion legislation is to alter their charters ?

Hon. Mr. ROSS.—I do not contend that the Act by which the Dominion Government assumed control of our railways contains any provisions which change the conditions upon which these charters were granted, but when the Dominion Government assumed to take control of these roads, they have assumed the power, without the consent of the Provincial legislatures, to change the conditions imposed in those charters as they see fit. (Hear, hear.) These conditions were imposed by this Province in consideration of the aid given to the railways, and now the views and opinions of the people of this Province may be over-ridden by the views of representatives of other Provinces in the Dominion Parliament. This is where I say the wrong is done. They assumed to control these railways, and take them out of the hands of the Provinces, taking upon themselves the power to change, or to wipe out of existence altogether, the conditions upon which the grants were made.   Now, I say that by the Act of 1882 the Dominion Government took upon themselves for the first time the burden and responsibility of extending aid to the construction of future local lines, because it was unreasonable to suppose that any Provincial Government would any longer continue to aid roads over which they had no jurisdiction or control, therefore I say that action of the Dominion Government in assuming these provincial roads put the Dominion Government in a new relation to the Provinces. They assumed all responsibility for aid to local roads, and put it out of the power of the Provinces to extend such aid themselves. But they did more.   When they assumed those roads in that manner, they rendered themselves, if not legally, morally and equitably, liable to the Provinces and the municipalities for a reimbursement of the aid that had been given, or at least for such a proportion as would represent that general interest of the Dominion which the Act affirmed.   Now, what was the ground upon which Quebec got this grant of $2,394,000 last year?   It was upon the ground that the Quebec and Ottawa Railway was a work of national, not merely of local interest.   But that is precisely the very same ground upon which they have assumed the jurisdiction of our roads.   That assumption was based upon powers given under sec. 92 of the B. N. A. Act, by which the Dominion are entitled to declare any work, though it be within the Province, to be of general interest to the Dominion; taking that ground, they have assumed the whole control of our roads, and by their Act have declared that all these roads that we have aided are not merely of local importance but are of general advantage to the Dominion.   If so, then, the liability of the Dominion follows at once to reimburse to the Provinces the aid given to secure the construction of these Dominion works.   That liability has been recognized in the case of the Province of Quebec; upon the same principle the Province of Ontario is in equity entitled to a portion of the amount it has expended on roads, which have, by the action of the Dominion, been declared to be for the benefit of the Dominion?

Mr. CARNEGIE.—What is the name of the local road in Quebec that the hon. gentleman speaks of?

Hon. Mr. ROSS.—I refer to the road from Quebec to Ottawa. It was constructed by the Province as a provincial work, they had expended $11,000,000 in constructing that road. In 1882 the Provincial Government made a proposition to the Dominion Government to buy that road from them. They offered it to the Dominion for the sum of $7,000,000, and in introducing the resolution into the Quebec Legislature, authorizing the sale to the Dominion, if they would accept it on these terms, the Attorney-General of the Province used this language. He said, " Let the Federal Government buy our property for $7,000,000. This would represent a loss to the Province of $4,000,000, but Quebec is willing to make a sacrifice which would ensure it an independent line for the traffic of the C. P. R., and at the same time give great impulse to the commerical prosperity of the Province," so that in 1882 the people of Quebec were willing to lose $4,000,000 of what they expended because they said they had received value for it as a provincial and local work. The Dominion refused to purchase the road on those terms, but it was sold afterwards, partly I believe to the C. P. R., and partly to another syndicate, for the sum of $7,600,000, or $600,000 more than they had offered it to the Dominion Government for, but there had been some improvements made upon it in the meantime. The loss to the Province on that transaction was $4,000,000. They had declared in 1882 that they were willing to submit to that loss, but last year, taking advantage of the opportunity which the demands of the C. P. R. upon the Government gave them, they insisted as a price of their support to that measure, that the Dominion Government should return them a portion of that money. The Dominion Government, feeling that the demand was one they could not at that time safely resist, gave Quebec $2,394,000 as a reimbursement in part of its grant to that road. I say that in all justice, in all equity, we, and all the other Provinces who have made similar grants to railways that are declared by the Dominion Government to be for the general advantage of Canada, and which that Government has taken under its control, are entitled also to a return of a portion of what we have granted for similar works. Even-handed justice must be extended to all the Provinces if our confederation is to continue. We cannot go on in this way, allowing other Provinces to receive benefits by special pleas of this kind, and the Province of Ontario get no equivalent. If our confederation is a partnership, then unless all the partners are accorded equal justice, that partnership cannot continue. I am satisfied that it only requires a united stand to be taken by the people of this Province and by the other Provinces, to ensure that the Dominion Government will return to us a portion of the amount we have expended, as they have done in the case of Quebec.

It being six o'clock, the Speaker left the chair.

After recess, Hon. Mr. Ross resumed:

Mr. SPEAKER, when the House adjourned, I was referring to the claim which I thought the Province had against the Dominion Government in regard to railways. I took the position, and still maintain that if our union is going to be continued, it must be upon a basis of equal justice to all; it must be upon the common ground that where special grants in the way of relief, which are but increased subsidies in disguise, are made to one province, similar advantages must be extended to the others also. The people will not consent that the partnership shall continue to exist if Ontario, being the largest contributing partner, is to be ignored in the distribution of the assets. Hon. gentlemen opposite adopted last year the statement that Ontario contributes from two-thirds to three-fourths of the revenue of the Dominion, but even supposing that she contributes only one half, of the $2,400,000 given to Quebec in the manner I have stated, Ontario will be called upon to pay $1,200,000—is it reasonable that she should be bound to contribute $1,200,000 in order to return to Quebec the aid that Province has given to a local road, and be refused herself a dollar in consideration of the roads which she has similarly aided, and which are declared to be as much Dominion roads as the one in the other Province—I do not think it is. I have a statement prepared here as to the amount of aid given by the Province for those roads assumed by the Dominion, taken over and now called Dominion roads. In the statements heretofore submitted of municipal aid, there has only been included, so far as I have seen, the municipal aid that has been given since 1873. Prior to that, before the settlement of the Municipal Loan Fund scheme, large aid had been granted by the municipalities to many roads. In the statement I will submit to the House I have included the aid extended by the municipalities to the roads before that date. By that scheme, also, the Province made expenditures in regard to local roads, by reimbursing to the municipalities a portion of the outlay they themselves had made. I take that into account as Provincial aid granted and paid towards these lines. I have also a statement shewing what has been contributed by each county towards the roads within that county, and also shewing the total amounts, both provincial and municipal, that have been given to the different lines of railway. Although it may take a little time, I will read it over to the House, as it will be of interest to the public and to the members representing the different localities. (See Schedule at end.)

I have given in this table the total amount of aid that has been given to every railway in the Province; every mile of these railways has been taken over by the Dominion. We have not a single mile of railway left over which the Province has control.

Mr. MEREDITH.—Yes, two miles and a-half.

Hon. Mr. Ross.—Oh, two miles and a-half, are there? We ought to be thankful for small mercies. These statements have been made up from the returns of municipal aid in the Dominion Sessional Papers of 1882.

It will be seen that there has been given a total municipal

aid of $12,624,849, and a total Provincial aid of $7,967,084, or a total municipal and Provincial aid of $20,591,952.

I come now to the estimated receipts for the current year, which I will read to the House.

ESTIMATED RECEIPTS, 1885.

Subsidy..		$1,196,872 80
Interest on capital held and debts due by the Dominion		
to Ontario..	$279,111 10	
Interest on investments...............................	50,000 00	
		329,111 10
CROWN LANDS DEPARTMENT :—		
Crown Lands.....................................	$115,000 00	
Clergy Lands.....................................	12,000 00	
Common School Lands........................	21,000 00	
Grammar School Lands.........................	2,000 00	
Woods and Forests............................	450,000 00	
		600,000 00
PUBLIC INSTITUTIONS :—		
Toronto Lunatic Asylum.........................	$32,000 00	
London "	10,000 00	
Kingston "	4,000 00	
Hamilton "	5,000 00	
Orillia "	2,000 00	
Reformatory for Females........................	5,000 00	
" Boys............................	500 00	
Central Prison..................................	32,000 00	
Deaf and Dumb Institute	500 00	
		91,000 00
Education Department..............................	$37,000 00	
" (School of Practical Science)....	1,000 00	
		38,000 00
Casual Revenue.....................................		34,000 00
Licenses..		168,000 00
Law Stamps..		66,000 00
Algoma Taxes......................................		10,000 00
Drainage Assessment...............................		25,000 00
Municipal Loan Fund...............................		10,000 00
Mechanics' Institute, Toronto......................		6,165 00
Insurance Companies' Assessments		3,000 00
Assessment of Counties re Removal of Lunatics.....		6,000 00
Agriculture and Arts Association re Agricultural Hall...		2,000 00
Total..		$2,585,148 90

Now hon. gentlemen will notice a considerable reduction in the amount we expect to receive from licenses. Last year our estimate was $200,000; we received $211,000. This year we estimate to receive only $168,000. This reduction is partly due to the adoption of the Scott Act in a number of the counties of the Province, which of course will reduce our revenues from licenses. I may mention that the estimated reduction by the adoption of the Act in these counties amounts to $24,091. Last year also we received $10,403 from extra licenses issued by the Dominion Commissioners, but as that Act has been declared *ultra vires*, we cannot expect any revenue from that source this year.

I may mention also that you will see in the estimates of this year the sum of $2,000 in connection with Agriculture and Arts and Agricultural Hall. Since last session a settlement has been made with the Agricultural and Arts Association in regard to the claim the Province had against them. We have agreed to accept from the Association the sum of $4,000, in two yearly instalments, as payment of the claim we had against them, the Association giving us an assignment of the claims that they may have against Mr. Jamieson for the proportion that he may have to pay towards the improvements that were made to the premises, and also a guarantee to the Province of ten years' use of the rooms now occupied by the Provincial Board of Health and Bureau of Statistics, so that in making this settlement we get $4,000 from the Association, the rooms that we occupy for these two branches and the Agricultural Department rent free for ten years, besides the assignment of any claims against Mr. Jamieson.

Now it will be seen by hon. gentlemen who have the estimates in their hands, that this estimate of receipts does not cover our estimated expenditure. In the statement made last year there was a deficiency also, and it may be as well to acknowledge that we have now arrived at that point when we cannot expect to meet all the demands that are made upon the Government and continue the liberal relief we have been extending to the municipalities out of our ordinary revenue. If the Government is to continue that liberality it must seek some additional sources of revenue. The Province is growing in population. Every year

D

there are new demands made upon the Government ; new outlets
spring up.   Either through municipalities or associations, representations are made to the Government, and where they show
that the proposed expenditures are in the public interest, the
Government ought to be in a position to grant them.   We have
thought that at present, having a considerable surplus on hand,
we should take any deficiencies out of the surplus rather than
shift any of our burdens upon the municipalities.   We therefore
estimate that there will be an excess of expenditures over receipts
in 1885.

Last year I drew the attention of the House to the fact that
although our population had increased largely since Confedera-
ation and a consequently largely increased expenditure forced
upon us, our revenue from the Dominion, which was intended
mainly to meet that expenditure, remains stationary ; and I said
there was a great deal of force in the contention that the subsidies to the Provinces ought to increase as population increases.
Since last session I think circumstances occurring at Ottawa
have confirmed my impression that it is just and right that the
subsidies should be rearranged on that basis.   Within the past
year several Provinces have made demands upon the Dominion
Government for increases under various pretexts.   We know
that the Province of Quebec, as I have already stated, sought
from the Dominion Government $2,394,000 on the plea that they
had constructed and given aid to a line of railway in the interest
of the Dominion.   We have seen that they forced acquiescence in
that demand.   We have seen, during the summer, Manitoba
sending a deputation to Ottawa asking for an increase of subsidy.
We have seen within the last two weeks a deputation from Nova
Scotia, also putting forward claims upon the Dominion Government and asking for an increase of subsidy.   We also know that
there are several Provinces now indebted to the Dominion
Government for advances.   The Province of New Brunswick has,
I believe, drawn its subsidy a year in advance.   We know from
past experience, when demands of this kind are unitedly pressed

—and there is union on such questions in other Provinces, although not in Ontario—they are always successful. Is it not time then that Ontario should take firm ground for some final arrangement that will do equal justice to all. It will not do to go on as we have been doing. The financial basis of Confederation is not giving satisfaction. The proof of that is that these other Provinces have been coming to the Dominion Government from time to time pressing these claims, which are merely increases of subsidy in disguise, and persuading the Dominion Government to accede to them. I say this system of special grants is pernicious and demoralizing in its effects. What is the result of it? What is its tendency? Is it not to encourage in the Provinces an ignoring of the responsibilities for the future, and a more ready acquiescence in present extravagant expenditures, feeling that the Dominion is at their back and bound to relieve them when they get into difficulties. I say that this has a tendency to lead to improvidence in the Provinces, and that it is time that we ought to have a final readjustment of the financial basis of Confederation, putting it upon some permanent ground that would give relief and at the same time take away from the Provinces the inducement to extravagant expenditures. That should be sought by some means that would do justice to all. Looking at all the circumstances, I believe that the fairest basis of revision would be the readjustment of the subsidies every ten years on the basis of population. That basis of population was adopted as the most equitable at Confederation. Population and expenditure are closely connected. The expenditure of a Province increases as the population increases, but under our present system that increase brings no additional revenue to the Province, but it does to the Dominion. It is from that source their principal revenue is derived. Increased population means increased consumption of dutiable goods which swells their customs receipts. We spend large sums yearly on immigration. Every additional immigrant brings additional revenue to the Dominion, but the Province does not participate in it. The

Dominion derives all the benefits in a revenue point of view, and the Province none ; on the contrary, an increased expenditure is thrown upon it. The administration of justice, schools, hospitals and charities, the care of the insane,—all these expenditures must be increased with the population.

Now, at the time' of confederation, a division was made as between the Provinces and the Dominion. What were the total revenues in 1867 of the four Provinces which went into confederation ? $13,687,928, and of that they apportioned to the Provinces, for the purpose of carrying on the local government, $2,753,966. It was considered right, then, to make the division so that the Provinces should receive one-fifth, and the Dominion the other four-fifths. What is the position of affairs now ? We find that the Dominion revenue in 1884 was $31,861,961. They gave as subsidies to the Provinces $3,606,672, or only one-ninth of the total revenue in 1884, though it had been considered an equitable division in 1867 to give the Provinces one-fifth. (Hear, hear.) Then, looking at the matter purely as regards items of revenue that are taxation ; that is, the revenue that the Dominion derives from customs and excise. From these two main branches of taxation, direct or indirect, as you may call them, was derived in the four Provinces in 1867, $11,580,968. In 1884 the Dominion derived from these same Provinces for customs and excise $23,711,745, or an increase of taxation of $12,130,777, but of that increase they gave the Provinces nothing. The Dominion grasped the whole. Is that equitable or fair ? Then, as it might be objected that these particular years, 1867 and 1884, do not properly represent the true proportion between now and then, I have taken the average of the first three years of Confederation and the last three years, from 1867 to 1869, and 1882 to 1884, taking the two larger Provinces of Ontario and Quebec alone, the total amount derived from customs and excise in the first three years was $9,774,987. They are now collecting by increased taxation from these two Provinces, $21,345,789.

Mr. MEREDITH.—That was Mr. Norquay's argument.

Hon Mr. Ross.—If it was, it is a good argument. I believe it would be in the interests of Manitoba, as well as in the interests of Ontario and Quebec to have some final settlement made. The hon. gentleman's remark merely confirms what I have stated that dissatisfaction is existing in all the Provinces regarding the basis of Confederation. But if the other Provinces have reason to complain, Ontario has more reason, for on various pretexts the other Provinces have got special increases, when no equivalent was given to Ontario. While on the only occasions on which Ontario has received anything from the Dominion, it was only in conjunction with full equivalents given to the other Provinces at the same time. Last year when they gave Quebec an increase, did they give Ontario an equivalent? Not at all.

Then with regard to the proportion per head of population. In 1867 the taxation from these two sources of customs and excise was $3.74; in 1884 it was $5.86 per head, and the Dominion absorbs the whole of this large increase and gives none to the Provinces except what has been given in 1873 and this last year. As some new basis, that will be a finality, must evidently be sought, I suggest, as an equitable one, that the Dominion subsidy should be increased every ten years, according to the population at the decennial census; no Province then would be able to find fault Each one would get a share in proportion to its population, and an increase as that population increases. No more equitable basis could be devised, because, as I stated before, it is largely from the increase of the population that the Dominion derives its increased revenue, and largely from increased population that increased expenditure is forced upon the Provinces The Provinces cannot go on providing for the increasing wants of the population if their revenues are to remain stationary.

An Hon. MEMBER.—How do the states of the Union do?

Hon. Mr. FRASER.—They impose direct taxation.

Hon. Mr. Ross.—They impose taxation, but I say, is it fair that the Dominion Government, starting upon what was supposed to be an equitable division of the revenues at the time confederation was formed, should go on doubling the taxation of the Provinces, taking the whole increase themselves, and allowing the Provinces only the resort to direct taxation ? What I object to is that the present system of granting specific sums to particular Provinces, whenever they are pressed with sufficient persistance, has a demoralizing tendency and leads to extravagant expenditure. They know that if they can bring any political influence to bear upon the Dominion Government, they can obtain relief from their embarrassments. I do not care if you cut off the subsidies from the Provinces altoether, and leave them to direct taxation, so long as you deal with them all equally and alike. But I say that so far as the Dominion Government are concerned, they are not merely content to leave our revenue stationary, while their own is increasing largely, but they endeavor by all the means in their power to reduce the revenue given to us by confederation. Have they not endeavored to take from us our license revenues that we have been in possession of since confederation ?

An Hon. MEMBER.—No, no.

Hon. Mr. Ross.—What was the McCarthy Act ? Does it not take away from us the revenues from wholesale and vessel and druggists' licenses and fines ? I think that is the intention. (Hear, hear.) I shall be very glad to hear that the Dominion Government make no such contention, and I hope the hon. gentleman is now expressing himself intelligently, and with fore-knowledge of what are the views of the Dominion Government on that question.

Now, Mr. Speaker, so far, the Provincial Government, notwithstanding these disabilities under which the Province has been labouring, have been able to meet the existing demands of the Province, and still we have a surplus in our treasury which will enable us to meet anything but extraordinary demands for a few years to come. But if we have, by economy and the wise administration of our finances, placed ourselves in a better position than some of the other Provinces, it is not right that that should be cast up to us as a reason why grants should be given to other Provinces and denied to us. (Hear, hear.) I say that it is useless for Ontario to stand idly by while other Provinces are coming successively to the Dominion and asking, under various pretexts and specious pleas, for increased subsidies, which, in every instance, taking advantage of opportunities, they have succeeded in getting. I say it is time for the Province to take a more united stand in regard to this. I am sorry to say that there seems to be in the people of this Province a lack of that local patriotism, that loyalty to their own Province, that characterizes the people of the other Provinces, that has enabled them, by their united patriotism, to secure a recognition of their demands. This is, perhaps, due to the doctrines that have been assiduously preached lately in Ontario, that the first and highest allegiance of the people is due to the Dominion and not to the Province. That when representations have been made of the injustice done to the Province of Ontario by the Dominion action, whether in the attempted robbery of her territory, the alienation of her revenues, or the infringement of her legislative rights, we have seen those who aspire to be leaders, in rounded phrases, reminding the people that they are building up a grand Dominion, and that Provincial interests are only of secondary consideration. What has been the result of that doctrine? Had we not the spectacle last year at Ottawa, that, when a proposition was made to do justice to Ontario, by returning to her as had been done to another Province, a portion of the aid given to construct Dominion roads, that proposition, although generally supported by Liberal members of other Provinces, was, for party ends, voted down by the voices of Ontario representatives. (Hear, hear.) It is time that Ontario assumed a firmer and more united attitude in assertion of her rights; and I trust she will, by united voice, demand the same recognition of her outlay on Dominion railways that has been accorded to other Provinces, and insist on an equitable and final adjustment of the basis of Confederation, both financially and constitutionally, which will give her that justice which the practical working out of the present arrangement as at present administered, does not secure to her. (Applause.)

Mr. Speaker, I beg to move that you do leave the chair.

STATEMENT X.

SUMMARY, shewing total Municipal (and Provincial) Aid to each Railway.

RAILWAY.	Amount of Bonuses. $ c.	Amount repaid by Province out of M.L.F. $ c.	Net amount of aid by County. $ c.	Direct aid by Province paid and maturing. $ c.	Total Provincial and Municipal aid to each Railway. $ c.
Buffalo and Lake Huron	1,278,000 00	322,000 00	956,000 00	.....	1,278,000 00
Bytown and Prescott	324,000 00	108,000 00	216,000 00	.....	324,000 00
Berlin and Preston	220,000 00	88,000 00	132,000 00	.....	220,000 00
Brockville and Ottwa (C.P.R.)	1,354,000 00	173,000 00	1,181,000 00	.....	1,354,000 00
Canada Atlantic	130,000 00	.....	130,000 00	454,887 00	584,887 00
Canada Central (C.P.R.)	117,500 00	.....	117,500 00	125,957 00	243,457 00
Canada Southern	322,500 00	.....	322,500 00	244,559 00	567,059 00
Credit Valley (C.P.R.)	1,085,000 00	.....	1,085,000 00	815,602 00	1,900,602 00
Cobourg, Peterboro' and Marmora	613,500 00	64,000 00	549,500 00	18,740 00	632,240 00
Erie and Niagara	306,000 00	61,000 00	245,000 00	.....	306,000 00
Grand Trunk, Georgian Bay and Lake Erie	929,000 00	.....	929,000 00	229,886 00	1,158,886 00
Galt and Doon	25,000 00	6,000 00	19,000 00	.....	25,000 00
Galt and Guelph	180,000 00	31,000 00	149,000 00	.....	180,000 00
Grand Junction	208,000 00	.....	208,000 00	278,067 00	486,067 00
Hamilton and North-Western	775,596 00	.....	775,596 00	727,697 00	1,503,293 00

Kingston and Pembroke	1,078,333 00	590,333 00	4900 00	....	488,000 00
London, Huron and Bruce	580,339 00	268,839 00	311,500 00	....	311,500 00
London, and Port Stanley	569,400 00	....	20,500 00	49, 000	569,400 00
Lake Simcoe Junction	153,000 00	53,000 00	100,000 00	....	100,000 00
Midland	360,391 00	215,511 00	122,870 00	22, 0000	144,870 00
Northern	787,128 00	155,148 00	631,980 00	....	631,980 00
Prince Edward County	249,020 00	155,520 00	3,500 00	....	93,500 00
Peterborough and Port Hope	1,100,000 00	....	942,000 00	158,000 00	1,100,000 00
Toronto, Grey and Bruce (C.P.R.)	1,449,364 00	461,364 00	916,000 00	72,000 00	988,000 00
Toronto and Nipissing	491,712 00	105,212 00	4301 00	41,999 00	386,500 00
Victoria	723,317 00	537,317 00	186,000 00	....	186,000 00
Wellington, Grey and Bruce	39276 00	241,276 00	634,002 00	47,998 00	682,000 00
Welland	190,000 00	....	97,000 00	93,000 00	9000 00
Whitby, Port Perry and Lindsay	13590 00	9290 00	222,000 00	....	222,000 00
Hamilton and Lake Erie	66,960 00	66,960 00	....	....	....
Prince Arthur's Landing	75,747 00	75,747 00	....	....	....
North Grey	41,040 00	41,040 00	....	....	....
Port Dover and Lake Huron	1900 00	3900 00	....	....	....
North Simcoe	144,241 00	144,241 00	....	....	....
Brantford, North, and South Brantford	9353 00	129,353 00	....	....	....
Belleville and North Hastings	114,206 00	4206 00	....	....	....
Erie and Huron	123,834 00	123,834 00	....	....	....
	20,591,952 00	6,630,086 00	12,624,849 00	1,336,997 00	13,961,846 00

STATEMENT shewing amount of Municipal Aid to Railways by various Counties in the Province of Ontario.

COUNTY.	RAILWAY.	Amount of Bonus. $	Amount repaid by Province out of Municipal Loan Fund. $	Net amount of Aid by County. $
Bruce......	Grand Trunk, G. Bay & Lake Erie	195,000		
	London, Huron & Bruce	9,000		
	Toronto, Grey & Bruce	43,000		
	Wellington, Grey & Bruce	306,000	4,363	
	Buffalo & and Lake Huron	53,571	20,809	581,399
Brant	Buffalo and Lake Huron	590,000	89,335	500,665
Carleton	Canada Atlantic	100,000		
	Bytown & Prescott	200,000	67,826	232,174
Dufferin	Credit Valley......	15,000		
	Toronto, Grey & Bruce	90,000	13,500	91,500
Elgin	Canada Southern	3,000		
	London & Pt. Stanley	114,000	13,493	

County	Railway			
	Credit Valley	50,000		375,507
Essex	Canada Southern	45,000		45,000
Frontenac	Kingston & Pembroke	488,000		488,000
Grey	Canada Southern	15,000		
	Grand Trunk, G. B. & L. E.	72,000		
	Northern	99,480		676,480
	Toronto, Grey & Bruce	305,000		17,122
Haldimand	Buffalo & Lake Huron	28,000	10,878	
Halton	Credit Valley	100,000		
	Hamilton & N. Western	87,080		187,080
Hastings	Grand Junction	165,000		175,000
	Prince Edward County	10,000		
Huron	London, Huron & Bruce	187,500		
	Toronto, Grey and Bruce	45,000		
	Wellington, Grey & Bruce	121,000		
	Buffalo & Lake Huron	62,429	95,716	504,213
Haliburton	Victoria	54,000		54,000
Leeds and Grenville	Bytown & Prescott	124,000	40,174	
	Brockville & Ottawa	1,354,000	173,000	1,264,826
Lincoln	Erie & Niagara	280,000	45,750	
	Welland	1000	93,000	331,250

STATEMENT shewing amount of Municipal Aid, etc.—*Continued.*

County.	Railway.	Amount of Bonus. $	Amount repaid by Province out of Municipal Loan Fund. $	Net Amount of Aid by County. $
Middlesex	London, Huron & Bruce (County)	15,000	....	....
	London, Huron & Bruce (City)	100,000	....	....
	London and Pt. Stanley	455,400	35,507	534,893
Norfolk	Canada Southern	30,000	....	....
	Grand Trunk, G. B. & L. E.	25,000	....	....
	Hamilton & N. Western	20,740	....	75,740
Northumberland and Durham	Grand Junction	39,000	....	....
	Cobourg, P. & Marmora	613,500	64,000	....
	Midland	30,000	....	....
	Peterboro' & Port Hope	920,000	132,145	1,406,355
Ontario	Midland	62,500	22,000	....
	Whitby, Pt. Perry & Lindsay	137,000	....	....
	Toronto & Nipissing	110,000	11,953	275,547

County	Railway			
Oxford	Canada Southern	7,500		
	Credit Valley	210,000		
	Grand Trunk, G. B. & L. Erie	130,000		347,500
Peel	Credit Valley	115,000		
	Hamilton & N. Western	30,974		
	Toronto, Grey & Bruce	85,000	12,750	218,224
Perth	Grand Trunk, G. B. & L. E.	225,000		
	Wellington, Grey & Bruce	50,000	5,454	
	Buffalo & Lake Huron	300,000	81,956	487,590
Peterboro'	Grand Junction	4,000		
	Midland	4,000		
	Peterboro' & Pt. Hope	100,000	14,364	93,636
Prescott and Russell	Canada Atlantic	30,000		30,000
Prince Edward	Prince Edward County	83,500		83,500
Renfrew	Canada Central	117,500		117,500
Simcoe	Hamilton & N. Western	537,069		
	Midland	46,370		
	Northern	242,500		825,939
Victoria	Midland	2,000		
	Victoria	132,000		
	Whitby, Port Perry & Lindsay	85,000		

STATEMENT shewing amount of Municipal Aid, etc.—*Concluded.*

County.	Railway.	Amount of Bonus.	Amount repaid by Province out of Municipal Loan Fund.	Net Amount of Aid by County.
		$	$	$
Victoria—(*Continued*)	Toronto & Nipissing	86,500	9,400	
	Peterboro' & Port Hope	80,000	11,491	364,609
Waterloo	Credit Valley	110,000		
	Galt & Doon	25,000	6,000	
	Galt & Guelph	40,000	7,294	161,706
Wellington	Credit Valley	135,000		
	Grand Trunk, G. B. & L. E.	97,000		
	Toronto, Grey & Bruce	70,000	8,250	
	Wellington, Grey & Bruce	205,000	38,181	
	Galt & Guelph	100,000	16,412	544,157
Welland	Buffalo & Lake Huron	60,000	23,306	
	Erie & Niagara	26,000	15,250	47,444
Wentworth	Hamilton & N. W	99,733		

Lightning Source UK Ltd.
Milton Keynes UK
UKHW010632161218
333983UK00010B/1149/P